Creating Business Plans

2Ⓞ MINUTE MANAGER SERIES

Get up to speed fast on essential business skills. Whether you're looking for a crash course or a brief refresher, you'll find just what you need in HBR's 20-Minute Manager series—foundational reading for ambitious professionals and aspiring executives. Each book is a concise, practical primer, so you'll have time to brush up on a variety of key management topics.

Advice you can quickly read and apply, from the most trusted source in business.

Titles include:

Creating Business Plans

Delegating Work

Finance Basics

Getting Work Done

Giving Effective Feedback

Innovative Teams

Managing Projects

Managing Time

Managing Up

Performance Reviews

Presentations

Running Meetings

20 MINUTE MANAGER SERIES

Creating Business Plans

Gather your resources
Describe the opportunity
Get buy-in

HARVARD BUSINESS REVIEW PRESS

Boston, Massachusetts

The web addresses referenced in this book were live and correct at the time of the book's publication but may be subject to change.

Library of Congress Cataloging-in-Publication Data

Creating business plans.
    pages cm. — (20-minute manager series)
  Includes index.
  ISBN 978-1-63369-580-1
1. Business planning.
  HD30.28.C7325 2014
  658.4'01—dc23

                2014000382

Preview

Writing a business plan is an important first step in starting any new venture. Your goal is to provide a detailed description of your new product or service and a concrete strategy for making it a success, while also conveying a hearty dose of enthusiasm that inspires investors and other supporters to want to be involved with your project. This book walks you through the basics:

- Articulating your business idea

- Communicating your goals

- Analyzing the industry

- Introducing your management team

Preview

- Distinguishing your business from rivals

- Developing a compelling marketing plan

- Describing your business's daily activities

- Providing sound financial projections

- Anticipating potential stumbling blocks

Contents

Contents

Creating Business Plans

Why Write a
Business Plan?

Why Write a Business Plan?

So you've got a brilliant idea for a new product or service. You feel energized, inspired, and ready to forge ahead. Your first challenge: Write a business plan.

You may be thinking: "Why should I bother taking the time to draft a formal plan? Shouldn't I just get going already?" If you're working at a large company and your boss asks you to put together a plan before you move forward with a new product extension, you may feel equally frustrated. "What's the point of this busywork?," you might think. "Why can't I just take the plunge?"

Don't fall into this trap. Writing a business plan for internal or external ventures is beneficial in a variety of ways, including gaining buy-in and generating enthusiasm for your idea, improving your odds of successfully creating a new product or service, establishing a company, raising capital, generating sales, and sustaining your business over time.

Whether you're planning to build a new company from scratch, expand an existing firm, spin off from a parent corporation, or even start an initiative within an established organization, writing a business plan gives you an opportunity to thoroughly evaluate your idea. It's also a way for your audience—namely potential investors, managers, and the people who control vital resources you need to start and operate your business—to assess the feasibility of your concept. Your goal is to create a road map for your business that helps you navigate the opportunities and inevitable obstacles you'll face and, perhaps most important, develop strategies to avoid problems before they arise.

This book shows you how to craft a persuasive argument for your idea by walking you through the elements of writing a business plan and providing a fully developed primary case study of an imaginary and hypothetical venture—TechnoExercise Corporation—which we'll follow throughout the chapters.

Getting started

Most business plans devote too much ink to numbers and too little to the information that matters most to potential investors, according to William Sahlman, a professor at the Harvard Business School and an expert in entrepreneurial ventures. After all, savvy investors understand that financial forecasts for a new company—particularly detailed, month-by-month projections that extend for years and years—are typically nothing more than wildly optimistic fantasies. In light of this, Sahlman recommends organizing your business plan around a framework that assesses four factors that are critical to every new venture:

- *The people.* Those who will be starting and running the business, in addition to any outside parties who will provide important resources.

- *The opportunity.* A profile of the business itself: what it will sell and to whom, whether it can grow and how quickly, what its economics are, and what might stand in the way of success.

- *The context.* The big picture—the regulatory environment, interest rates, demographic trends, inflation, and so on. Essentially, factors that inevitably change but that you cannot control.

- *The risk and reward.* An examination of everything that can go wrong and right, as well as a discussion of how the team can respond.

With Sahlman's four critical factors in mind, you're ready to start thinking about what information you'll gather to create the most compelling business plan you can. As you begin your research, ask yourself some important questions:

- *What's your purpose?* If your business plan is a proposal within the resource-rich environment of a large corporation, certain parts of it—such as the marketing or operations sections—could be shorter and less developed than other sections. In this case, you ought to focus on the value proposition and competitive analysis. On the other hand, if you're using the plan to raise money from venture capitalists, you ought to focus more on the opportunity itself and the management team.

- *Who's your audience?* Knowing who will be reading your plan and why and having some sense of their goals and needs will help you tailor your message. To learn about your audience's particular requirements and motivations, do some research. Tap your network—ask colleagues and other industry professionals for their views on the problem you're trying to solve. Also, think about your proposal from the perspective of your audience. A corporate management committee or board of directors, for instance, will consider your idea within the context of the company's other initiatives and may look for potential cost savings or other sales opportunities related to your idea. Investors and lenders, on the other hand, may want to know about the breakeven points and the business's longer-term potential.

- *What do you want?* Think about your ultimate goal. Do you need a corporate stamp of approval or the active support of upper management? Are you just looking for funding, or do you want connections with other investors or business partners? Do you want to repay a loan, or are you willing to share ownership and profits?

What information will you need?

Now that you've organized your thoughts, you need to determine whether you have all the relevant material on hand. Some of this will be financial and legal information. For example, have you confirmed the necessary production costs for your product? Have you considered the most appropriate legal structure and tax status for your business? There are many sources for this kind of information. You should identify trade journals that target business owners in your industry, seek out research by respected analysts, and scour your network for experts who may be able to help you develop a fuller picture of the business environment. Online resources are also available, including your local chamber of commerce's website and the official sites of the Small Business Administration, the Internal Revenue Service, the Census Bureau, and state departments of economic development.

The structure of a business plan

The most common business plan structure opens with short, general summaries (such as the executive summary and the business description) and then proceeds to more in-depth explanations in the body of the plan. That's where you'll provide thoughtful descriptions of your business's fundamental elements and concerns. The attachments at the end include the most detailed information—financial data, management résumés, and so forth.

Writing a business plan is a big undertaking that requires time, dedication, and discipline. Rather than tackling it all at once, go section by section. Dividing the task into manageable chunks will help you better plan your time. Throughout the process, seek input from others. Talk over your idea with mentors, business partners, and colleagues. Ask them to look for gaps in your plan or potential red flags. Then make adjustments as you go.

Most business plans contain the following components, which we'll cover in more detail throughout the book:

- *Cover page:* This ought to include the name of your business or project, as well as your name and contact information.

- *Table of contents:* An at-a-glance view of which topics will be covered. Use straightforward language to allow readers to easily skim or flip through to find what they're looking for.

- *Executive summary:* A brief and formal explanation of what your company is, where you want it to go, and why it will be successful.

- *Business description:* A high-level overview of your proposed venture.

- *Industry background:* Historical data as well as current information about the shape, size, trends, and key features of the industry.

- *Competitive analysis:* A breakdown of current and prospective rivals.

- *Market analysis:* Your assessment of your target customers and their wants, needs, and demographics.

- *Management summary:* An introduction to your team as well as a description of how they will work together to form an effective and successful unit.

- *Operations plan:* The flow of the business's daily activities and the strategies that will support them.

- *Marketing plan:* Your detailed strategy for how you intend to sell your product or service.

- *Financial plan:* A synopsis of the current status and future projections of the company's financial performance.

- *Attachments and milestones:* Additional documents that supply more detailed information about elements of the plan.

Of course, not all business plans follow this model precisely. As you'll see in the next chapter, your plan may combine some of these sections, add new ones, and eliminate others, based on your audience and its needs.

Describing the Opportunity

Describing the Opportunity

You know your idea inside and out, so it can be easy to lose sight of the details that will matter to investors when you draft your business plan. Ensure that your plan explains how your offering will help customers and places that offering within the larger business context, too.

Presenting your idea

Win readers over with a description of your idea that addresses a clear and specific business need and provides details about the larger context within which your offering will thrive.

To add customer focus to your plan, consider these questions as you define your product or service: What customer pain are you easing with your offering? What special technology, new perspective, or unique concept will you offer customers that is better than what's available now? And what will compel them to buy your product rather than your competitors'?

Even if you're not trying to raise a round of venture funding and are instead trying to build a persuasive case for a new product or initiative within your company, you must make sure the business need is clear. If your investors and managers don't agree with your explanation of the problem, they're not going to support your venture. Let's say, for instance, that you're trying to solve the problem of low customer usage of your company's mobile retail shopping app. You have an idea to redesign the app that could increase customer engagement. But what if the technologists at your company don't think there's anything wrong with the app? What if, instead, they believe that low customer usage is the result of poor marketing? To gain buy-in for your idea, you'd have to build a case for the technology group and other decision makers with evidence that proves that the root cause of low engagement is a design flaw, not a problem of branding or awareness.

Of course, you can't really describe your plan and its customer focus clearly without addressing the "context" in which your business will flourish. We'll explore that part later, in "Analyzing the business environment."

Executive summary

The *executive summary* is a concise description of what your company is, where you want it to go, and why it will be successful. In just one page, it gives readers an understanding of your proposal and captures their interest in your new venture. In some cases, this is the only section your time-pressed audience may read, so the key is to present your concept passionately

SAMPLE COVER PAGE

To give you a better sense of how a business plan might look, this book offers a primary case. Meet TechnoExercise Corporation ("TechEx"), an imaginary, hypothetical online diet and exercise service based in Cambridge, MA. Woven throughout this book, you'll find examples of certain sections of TechEx's business plan that will help you understand how it fits together. This is just one sample—there are many variations, since a good business plan is always tailored to its audience.

Here is the material that goes on the cover page:

TECHNOEXERCISE CORPORATION

TechEx

559 Treburke St.

Cambridge, MA 02115

(617) 555-1234

www.technoexercise.com

Ping Huang
Founder and Chief Executive Officer
email: pinghuang@techex.com
cell: (617) 555-8888

Anjali Banerjee
Chief Financial Officer
email: anjalibanerjee@techex.com
cell: (617) 555-2222

Mercedes Meceda
Chief Technology Officer
email: mercedesmeceda@techex.com
cell: (617) 555-7777

Plan prepared July 2014 by Corporate Officers

and lay out why you believe the business will be a re-sounding success, even as you acknowledge the risks and costs involved. A well-crafted executive summary will inspire your reviewers to read on.

Sketching out your executive summary can give you a rough idea of what you plan to say, but rewrite and polish it once you've finished drafting your entire business plan, paying attention to those areas that may have changed during the writing process.

An executive summary typically includes the following elements:

- A *mission statement*: one or two sentences that describe what your business is about, its philosophy, and your vision for its future.

- A succinct description of the industry and market environment in which your new venture will develop and flourish.

- An explanation of the unique business opportunity you'll be taking advantage of.

- A brief mention of the competitive advantages that differentiate your product or service from rivals' offerings.

- A rundown of the financial potential of your new venture, as well as the anticipated risks.

- A description of the management team and their respective roles.

- Information about the stage of the business (on the drawing board, in start-up mode, ready to expand), its financial status (whether you've raised any money or have taken out any loans for the business thus far), and its structure (partnership, corporation, affiliate). Online resources such as the website of the Small Business Administration will be very helpful here.

- Details on the capital requested so that readers understand what you hope to gain from them, such as money, contacts in the industry, or other resources.

SAMPLE EXECUTIVE SUMMARY

TechEx's mission: The driving principle of Techno-Exercise Corporation ("TechEx") is to change the way women lose weight and tone their bodies using four key elements: customized data-driven metrics, personal psychology, access to certified health professionals, and emotional support from a community.

How it works: Customers wear a stylish monitor (fitfast) that tracks their eating and exercise patterns online. They also receive one-on-one weekly video chat sessions with a registered dietician, behavior coach, and trainer, all of whom monitor their weight loss and muscle gain via a customer-supplied wireless scale. Through message boards, instant messaging software, and moderated chat rooms, customers also have access to a community of fellow dieters who provide them with emotional support and encouragement.

Structure: TechEx, which was incorporated under the laws of the State of California on August 30, 2013, is headquartered in Cambridge, MA, in the heart of the US entrepreneurial community. The company has filed a petition with the Internal Revenue Service seeking to qualify as an "S Corporation."

Market: The service appeals to busy professional women who don't have time for traditional fitness and weight loss programs. These women may be overweight and in search of diet plans, or they may already be at a healthy weight and looking to mix up their fitness routines. TechEx will promote its service through targeted advertisements in diet and fitness magazines. The company will expand its marketing activities through strategic alliances with employers and insurance plans as well as partnerships with healthcare groups and gyms.

(continued)

SAMPLE EXECUTIVE SUMMARY

Management team: The company's founder, Ping Huang, is a former operations manager at an online nutrition start-up. She met her business partners, Anjali Banerjee, who worked at Morgan Goldman investment bank in Dublin, Ireland, and Mercedes Meceda, a former Dain consultant, at MIT's Sloan School of Management. Together, this management team is responsible for TechEx's daily operations and owns 100% of the company.

Competitors: The weight loss industry is crowded and the market environment is highly competitive. TechEx's primary rival is E-Fitfab, a full-service program similar to TechEx. However, E-Fitfab does not have any element of community and social support, which research indicates is very important to female dieters. Other large, well-known weight loss companies, such as Calorie Counters and Jenny Haig, tend to focus more on healthy eating rather than exercise; furthermore, they are so big that they cannot offer customized services. Other competitors include free apps like MyExerciseBuddy and Lose Weight!, which help users track food and exercise while also networking with friends. These products are aimed at customers who take a DIY approach to diet and exercise, while TechEx is targeted at customers who prefer a tailor-made full-service program. In short, TechEx is the only company that offers customizable and convenient diet and exercise solutions combined with the social support critical to effective weight loss. Nonetheless, one of the biggest risks the company faces comes from potential me-too competitors who might exploit parts of TechEx's business model.

Pricing strategy: TechEx is priced below E-Fitfab, which will put it in square competition with that company, but TechEx's pricing still positions it as a first-class service provider.

(continued)

SAMPLE EXECUTIVE SUMMARY

Financial status: TechEx seeks funding of $250,000 that will add to the $84,000 of initial financing that was raised among friends and family. At this point, the biggest challenge that TechEx faces is cash flow. The company requires immediate funding for system development and technology programming as well as advances for contracts with dieticians, behavior coaches, and trainers. These represent TechEx's biggest costs.

What is TechEx's future? The company estimates first-year sales of $11.74 million, gross margins over 60%, and net margins of approximately 42% before taxes. The company expects to be profitable after the first six months of operations. After that, TechEx plans to embark on an international expansion plan in Europe. Ultimately, the management team would like to take the company public.

Business description

The *business description* is another summary, but it differs from the executive summary because it provides a high-level, forward-looking overview of your proposed venture. This is the section of the plan where you go into greater detail about your business. Think of it as an extended elevator pitch that helps readers and potential investors quickly grasp the concept of your business and its value proposition. The business description must also demonstrate how an opportunity can grow—in other words, how the new venture can increase its range of products or services, expand its customer base, or widen its geographic scope.

In some cases, your proposed product or service is so unusual or technical that it deserves its own separate section to explain what it is and how it functions. This will also highlight your venture's special features and points of differentiation from the competition.

SAMPLE BUSINESS DESCRIPTION

TechEx offers a distinctive blend of exercise and diet monitoring that combines cognitive behavioral approaches to weight loss using cutting-edge technologies. It is aimed at time-crunched women who either travel extensively for their jobs or have little time to get to the gym because of other demands in their lives. It provides three important benefits that address the target end user's needs: flexibility, support, and targeted weight loss.

The plan works like this: When a customer establishes an account, she receives a wearable and stylish fitfast monitor that tracks her eating and exercise patterns online. She is also granted access to a range of auxiliary services, including one-on-one weekly video chat sessions with a registered dietician, behavior coach, and trainer, each of whom keep track of her weight and progress via the fitfast monitor. (This increases the effectiveness of the program: According to a study in the *Archives of Internal Medicine*, patients in weight-loss treatment programs lost more weight when they coupled nutritional coaching and exercise with prompts from mobile apps.) The customer may also tap into a community of fellow dieters that provides her with social and emotional support through message boards, moderated chat rooms, and instant messaging software. The community also shares tips, including products, recipes, and ideas for how to keep fit while traveling.

TechEx's interface is user-friendly, and the service allows the client to configure packages that will meet her unique needs. For instance, customers can easily:

- Register and activate the product using nothing more than a credit card and mobile phone.

(continued)

SAMPLE BUSINESS DESCRIPTION

- Specify weight loss and/or fitness goals, and modify those numbers at any time.

- Enjoy one-on-one weekly video chat sessions with a registered dietician and a behavior coach.

- Discover exercise opportunities unique to their specific location, such as running routes in a foreign city or the best yoga class near home.

- Receive low-calorie meal suggestions for restaurants in any major metropolitan area.

- Check community boards for notes on spots that are friendly for a "table for one."

- Participate in weekly virtual personal workout sessions with a certified trainer, using small weights, bands, and other portable exercise tools.

- Customize exercise plans for targeted work on certain body parts, such as abdominals or arms.

- Review their weekly and monthly progress at any time.

- Engage with other members of the TechEx community as often as they choose.

TechEx also has plans to expand internationally. The first targets include Ireland and the United Kingdom, where obesity rates are on the rise and where a large number of professional women are in the workforce. There is additional long-term growth potential in other countries in Western Europe.

Analyzing the business environment

This section illustrates the potential of your idea within the context of its industry and market. We use the terms *industry* and *market* to describe separate but overlapping parts of the broader business environment. *Industry* refers to the group of companies that produce and sell products or services to the market. The *market* is where your product or service will be sold. The industry defines both your colleagues and your competitors; the market determines your opportunity and your customers. The area of intersection represents your business opportunity—that space in which the customer's need meets the product or service you provide.

To clarify the context for your opportunity, address these two questions: Is the market for your new product or service big, growing fast, or—ideally—both? And: Is the industry now, or can it become, structurally attractive—that is, where sales or demographic trends are favorable? Why does this context matter? As William Sahlman notes, investors seek out large or rapidly growing markets because getting a share of an expanding market is often easier than competing with established players for a share of a mature or declining market. Indeed, savvy investors try to spot markets with high growth potential early in their development because that's ultimately where the big payoffs are.

Start by demonstrating an awareness of your new venture's environment and how it helps or hampers your particular proposal. You should include information on the macroeconomic situation, as well as background on the range of government rules and regulations that will affect your plans. Such information is readily available from official government websites, trade association sites, and published news articles from reputable magazines and newspapers. Next, show that you understand that the venture's context will undoubtedly change and try to articulate how those changes might influence the business. Finally, describe how management will react if the context changes in an unfavorable way (see sidebar "Sample Industry Background").

A tip: As you research the industry background, competitive analysis, and market analysis sections, document your sources. Support your claims about market growth and competitive strategies with verifiable information and expert sources such as a market research firm, trade association, or credible journalist. Good record keeping will pay off in the short and long term.

Industry background

The first element of the business environment analysis is *industry background*, which provides details about the shape and size, as well as other important features, of the industry. The following questions will help frame your thinking:

- *What is the industry?* What are the products or services currently produced by the industry? How big is it? What is its overall profitability? What characteristics define the industry? What are its special challenges? Is the industry spread out geographically, or is it concentrated?

- *What is the industry's outlook?* What important trends are emerging? What is the industry's predicted growth rate? What factors might contribute to future growth? What new patterns of growth are emerging?

- *Who competes in this industry?* Is the industry fragmented, consisting of many small participants? Or are there a few major competitors controlling it? Which companies have offerings that meet the same needs as your proposed product or service? What resources do they control?

- *What are the industry's barriers to entry?*
  What is your window of opportunity to enter
  the market? What are the obstacles that could
  block you from entering this industry? What
  resources, knowledge, or skills does it take to
  enter this industry? Are there restrictive fed-
  eral or international regulations, large capital
  requirements, or areas of sophisticated technical knowledge associated with providing the
  products or services?

SAMPLE INDUSTRY BACKGROUND

The global weight loss and obesity management market—which is estimated to be worth $265 billion—
includes a wide variety of products and services in
three main categories: over-the-counter consumer
goods, such as diet beverages, low-calorie packaged
meals, and nutritional supplements; weight loss ser-

vices, such as structured diet plans; and fitness equipment and surgical procedures. Within this industry, TechEx competes as a weight loss service.

Market growth: Obesity rates are rising around the world, but the United States—which has the sixth highest rate of obesity in the world—remains the leading market for diet and exercise companies. The global increase in obesity and associated chronic diseases, namely diabetes and heart disease, are accelerating the growth of the industry. Other key factors driving growth include: rising disposable income, a pronounced stigma against excess weight, policy initiatives to raise awareness about the importance of health and fitness, and technological advancements that enable simple, expedient tracking of diet and exercise. In 2012, the weight loss industry as a whole grew at a steady 3% in the United States.

(*continued*)

SAMPLE INDUSTRY BACKGROUND

Industry landscape: The US diet and exercise industry is highly saturated; it includes several big, well-established players in addition to thousands of small competitors vying for a share. (See competitive analysis.) Most of these companies target female dieters, but thus far none have concentrated on the niche market of highly educated professional women. (See market analysis.)

Emerging trends: In the aftermath of the global financial crisis and the subsequent recession, dieters in the United States have recently gravitated toward free and/or inexpensive do-it-yourself diet plans. These include over-the-counter solutions such as diet pills and books, as well as online eating and exercise platforms and mobile apps. According to Marketdata Enterprises, the internet-based diet plan market is worth at least $1.1 billion and is growing at

8% per year. Customers seek online solutions because they're convenient, easy-to-use, and cost effective, but most online weight loss solutions are one-size-fits-all programs that do not work for all customers.

TechEx's unique selling point: The TechEx platform is highly attractive to professional women who are overweight as well as those who are in shape but looking to mix up their fitness routines. These women require personalized services tailored to their specific diet and exercise needs, and they want these services to be structured in a way that is convenient to their busy lives. This group tends to earn above-average incomes and demonstrate willingness to pay a premium for convenience. Such women are motivated and highly educated, and also predisposed to heed advice from experts. TechEx blends customized expertise with a

(continued)

SAMPLE INDUSTRY BACKGROUND

straightforward interface that customers can access at any time they wish.

Barriers to entry: Generally speaking, there are very few natural barriers to entry (such as capital requirements or proprietary technology) that would prevent new market entrants. Consequently, prospective competitors will likely develop and promote competing products once they learn of TechEx's success. Anticipating the threat of new market entrants, TechEx is forming strategic alliances with employer-based health and wellness programs to offer its services to employees who must travel frequently for their jobs. TechEx believes that these exclusive arrangements will effectively preclude potential competitors from reaching the target markets in a cost-competitive fashion. TechEx is seeking to establish a second barrier by creating a brand identity for its stylish fitfast wear-

████████████████████████████████

able monitor so that clients will come to recognize the TechEx brand as a reliable, high-quality service.

Sources: *The US Weight Loss & Diet Control Market* (Tampa, FL: Market-data Enterprises, April 2013); *Weight Loss and Obesity Management Market* (Dublin, Ireland: Research and Markets, May 2013); and CIA World Fact Book.

Competitive analysis

The second part of evaluating the business environment is a *competitive analysis*. In this section, you identify any direct and future competitors of your venture and describe the threats they represent to your success. Whether your target audience is potential investors or a corporate leadership board, your readers require that you thoughtfully appraise your current and potential rivals in order to weigh the viability of your idea.

Here are some questions to consider:

- *Who are your competitors?* Think in terms of which companies solve the same problems for the customer that you intend to. What are their products and services? How much market share does each competitor control? Consider that rival companies could exist in another industry. For instance, a competitor to TechEx might be a shapewear company. Customers may forgo paying for a diet and workout service and instead buy better foundation garments to look good.

- *What are your competitors' strengths and weaknesses?* Do they enjoy strong brand recognition of their products? What are their marketing strategies? What has been key to their profitability?

- *What distinguishes your business from rivals?* How are you responding to a customer need in a new and useful way? What differentiates your product or service from competitors' offerings?

- *What is the competitive outlook for the industry?* How much of a threat are your competitors to your venture? Will they aggressively block the entrance of a new rival? Will they poach your ideas, appropriating them for their own business (killing your unique value proposition)? Who else might be able to observe and exploit the same opportunity?

Market analysis

The final part of assessing the business environment is the *market analysis.* In this section, you focus on your target market—the group of people or companies that will choose to purchase and remain loyal to your product or service because you solve a problem or meet a need for them better than your rivals do. This is where you demonstrate that there is indeed an opportunity within this market and that your new venture can capitalize on it.

SAMPLE COMPETITIVE ANALYSIS

Industry competition for TechEx comes in several forms. But while the companies listed below represent some threat to TechEx, none offers precisely the same cognitive behavioral approach to sensible eating and exercise, while also providing crucial emotional and community support.

1. **E-Fitfab:** TechEx's closest rival is a full-service program in which customers wear a monitor that tracks their eating and exercise patterns. Its advantages are that customers have access to a registered dietician and a behavior coach. However, its biggest drawback is that E-Fitfab lacks any element of community, which research indicates is very important to women dieters. (Studies show that people derive satisfaction from an online weight loss community because it offers recognition for achievement,

accountability, friendly competition, and hu-mor. They also value non-judgmental interac-tions with others.) TechEx offers a wide range of online social support through its community of fellow dieters via message boards, chat rooms, and video conferencing software.

2. **Calorie Counters:** The 800-pound gorilla in the industry is perhaps the most recognized brand in the commercial weight loss world. The Calorie Counters program is based on account-ability and community support, à la Alcoholics Anonymous. Its main strength is that members are weighed weekly and attend meetings where they find encouragement from a community of fellow dieters. The company uses a system that assigns points to every food and members get

(*continued*)

SAMPLE COMPETITIVE ANALYSIS

a daily target number so they easily know how much they should eat in order to lose weight safely. Calorie Counters' biggest problem, however, is that it has been slow to adapt to new technologies. It does not, for instance, offer online meetings and provides limited internet-based support. Its system is very inconvenient for busy customers who are not able to make it to the meetings on a regular basis. Finally, Calorie Counters is so large that it cannot offer custom eating and exercise services, which is what many dieters so desperately need. By contrast, technology lies at the heart of the TechEx business model. TechEx's cutting-edge system enables customers to engage when it's easy and convenient for them.

3. **Jenny Haig:** Another industry powerhouse, Jenny Haig provides a program based on

restricting calories, fat, and portions using prepackaged meals. Members also receive weekly one-on-one counseling sessions with a Jenny Haig consultant. The company's strength lies in the fact that it makes eating well very easy for customers. However, the program is cost-prohibitive for many people, and it does not have enough variety for customers with special food allergies or dietary concerns. It's also too narrowly focused on the food aspect of weight loss. TechEx takes a holistic approach that blends psychology and physiology into a sensible eating and exercise program.

4. **Free apps:** Other competitors include free apps such as MyExerciseBuddy and Lose Weight!, which help users track food and exercise while also networking with friends. These products

(continued)

SAMPLE COMPETITIVE ANALYSIS

are free and geared at customers who take a DIY approach to diet and exercise. TechEx, on the other hand, is targeted at customers who prefer a tailor-made full-service program and who wish to receive support from health and fitness experts rather than just advice from friends.

Sources: "Social support in an internet weight loss community," NIH manuscript, January 2010, http://www.ncbi.nlm.nih.gov/pubmed/19945338 and "Dieting in the Digital Age," Knowledge@Wharton, October 2013.

If you're trying to start a new program or initiative at your company, you should begin by talking to colleagues who are directly affected by the problem and will consequently benefit from the solution. Ask them: When did the issue start? How does it manifest itself? Marshal relevant reports, surveys, and other evidence. This will help you develop a full picture of the issue so you can tweak your idea to better solve the problem.

Here are some other fundamental questions this section must address:

- *Who are your target customers?* How many of them are there? What is the forecasted growth for this group? Consider the target market from different perspectives, such as geographic location or segmentation (national, state, suburban, city, neighborhoods), demographic features (age, gender, race, income level, occupation, education, religion), and behavioral factors (customers' attitudes and responses to types of products).

- *What are your prospective customers' critical needs?* Are those needs being met? How does the customer make decisions about buying certain products or services? Are these purchase patterns affected by economic cycles or other seasonal factors? As Harvard Business School professor Clayton Christensen asks: What job is the customer hiring the product to do?

- *Why will customers in your target market purchase your product or service?* What are your solutions to customer problems? What customer discomfort will your product or service ease? How will your customers differentiate your product from those of your competitors?

SAMPLE MARKET ANALYSIS

Size of the US market: At any given time, there are approximately 108 million Americans on a diet. Typically, these people make four to five attempts per year to lose weight, spending $40 billion a year on weight-loss programs and products. Within the US weight loss industry—which will reach $66.5 billion in revenue this year—women are a special category, comprising

85% of customers. Women who purchase weight loss programs and products represent a large and growing demographic group with above-average income and a higher than average level of education. The number of women in the labor force is projected to be more than 78 million by 2018. Today, about 73% of those women have white-collar occupations, a percentage that is expected to increase.

Potential international market: As obesity rates climb internationally, diet programs are becoming more popular overseas. This is particularly true in Europe, where TechEx plans to expand. For instance, one recent study shows that some British women spend £25,233 on diets over the course of their lives.

Target customers: While Calorie Counters, which relies on a group meetings model, and Jenny Haig, which relies on meal replacement, have long been

(continued)

SAMPLE MARKET ANALYSIS

go-to companies for most women, they are steadily losing their appeal. Increasingly, many women are turning to technology-based diet plans, including diet websites and exercise apps, because they are more convenient for their busy lives.

Against this backdrop, TechEx offers a uniquely effective experience for two target end users:

Busy professional women who are overweight: A general characteristic of this group is that they lack time to make it to regular group meetings, let alone the gym. They are knowledgeable about, and have experimented with, most of the popular diet plans, but find them impractical for the realities of their lives. These women seek a solution that is convenient and has a measurable impact on their weight. As a group, they tend to be highly motivated and tech-savvy; when faced with a decision, they are moved by hard data and scientific evidence. They trust health professionals and regularly seek expert opinions. (For example, they trust fitness advice from a reputable and well-researched magazine rather than a late-night infomercial.) Because of their hectic work and home lives, they have experienced a sense of isolation because they don't have a community with which to share their struggles. They crave emotional support.

Busy women who are of a healthy weight but want to mix up their routines: These women are looking for ways to maintain their weight, but also improve their bodies and level of nutrition. They are highly motivated to make adjustments to their routines for the benefit of their health. They may work long hours or take time out of the workforce to care for young children or aging

(continued)

SAMPLE MARKET ANALYSIS

parents. Either way, they are unable to make it to the gym and instead need a program they can do at home or on the road. They are looking for a program that will tailor a fitness and nutrition regimen to their specific concerns (such as a flabby stomach or un-toned biceps), and one that will produce real results.

TechEx, with its emphasis on customization (based on personal data), expert support (from dieticians, psychologists, and trainers), convenience (all programs are delivered online/mobile), and emotional support (from a sisterhood of women who also struggle to create and maintain healthy lifestyles on the go) is a natural choice for these two groups.

Sources: US Department of Labor; MarketData Enterprises; National Weight Control Registry; *Bloomberg Businessweek*; Center for Disease Control; and Engage Mutual: http://www.engagemutual.com/about-us/media-centre/all-news/2010-press-releases/cost-of-dieting/.

Introducing Your Management Team

Introducing Your
Management Team

Ask seasoned investors what they think is the key to converting a solid business plan into a successful venture, and they will tell you: the people running it. Indeed, many investors say that the *management summary* is one of the first sections of a business plan they read. After all, it's the leadership team that makes a business work as a finely formed, dynamic unit. That team includes not only the men and women who start and run the venture, but also the outside parties who provide important services or resources for it, such as lawyers, accountants, and suppliers, in addition to any people who serve as advisors or directors. If your audience is in-ternal—the upper management of your division, for example—this section is an opportunity to show how your proposed team will work together to take on new responsibilities.

Without the right team, no business idea will move from concept to reality. Your goal in the management summary section, therefore, is to extol the virtues of this team while providing answers to these three questions: What do they know? Whom do they know? And finally: How well are they known?

Highlighting qualifications

Your management team's résumés will be included in the attachments portion of your business plan, so use the biographical section to call out select aspects of their professional paths that are related to your venture:

- *Where have your team members worked?* How much experience do they have? Who are their contacts in your target or related industries? What work have they done that relates directly to this proposed business?

- *What have they accomplished?* Where did they go to school? What are their achievements? Do they have a proven track record? What knowledge, skills, and special abilities do they bring to the business?

- *What is their reputation in the business community?* Are they known for their integrity? Do they have a reputation for being hardworking or especially dedicated to their work?

- *Are they realistic about the business's chances for success?* Are they capable of recognizing risks and responding to problems that arise? Do they have the courage to make the hard decisions that inevitably have to be made? Who on the team is a visionary? Who will offer words of caution?

- *How committed are they to this venture?* What motivates them? What do they hope to achieve? What benefits do they wish to gain? For ventures within an established organization, indicate whether the members of the team are there by choice or because they've been assigned to the project. If they've been assigned, what tools will the team use to motivate them to see the project through successfully?

Presenting the team as a unit

Use this section to describe how each of the team members will work to form an effective unit, which will in turn result in a successful and profitable business. This is your opportunity to demonstrate that your team is the right one to manage risks and capitalize on potential opportunities.

- *Affirm the team's strengths.* Describe how the skills, knowledge, and experience of the individual members balance the team as a whole. Note what each member will bring to the table (legal expertise, great vendor relationships).

- *Acknowledge and address the team's perceived weaknesses.* Investors and other backers want to see a team that has a history of overcoming internal conflicts and external problems to meet a goal. An untested team is generally considered a riskier proposition than a group that has worked together in the past. If management gaps exist, such as technical skills or marketing experience, explain how you'll address those weaknesses. If no team members have strong financial backgrounds, for example, clarify that you've enlisted the services of an accounting firm.

- *Describe the team's management philosophy.* Develop a set of guidelines to help steer each member's behavior and decision making. A clear statement of management philosophy is an expression of company values and provides an example of the team's cohesiveness. Think about your team's guiding principles and leadership style. Reflect on how you make decisions, set goals and expectations, and measure quality. Consider how you believe customers and employees should be treated.

SAMPLE MANAGEMENT SUMMARY

Partners: The management team comprises Ping Huang, the founder, and two other top leaders: Anjali Banerjee and Mercedes Meceda.

Huang, founder and CEO of TechEx, has relevant personal and professional experience. A Chinese national, she immigrated to the United States when she was 18 to study mathematics at UCLA. In college, she was active and maintained a healthy weight. After graduation, however, she started working in jobs that required significant travel. She couldn't get to the gym and often found herself eating off the room service menu at chain hotels. In one year, she gained 30 pounds. She tried a myriad of diet and exercise plans; nothing worked, mainly because the plans were either inconvenient or not suited to her needs. Finally, she contacted a cognitive behavioral expert and started working remotely

(continued)

SAMPLE MANAGEMENT SUMMARY

with a trainer and a dietician. She saw immediate re-sults. She thought: "If only I could find a way to scale these services." She arrived at MIT Sloan determined to make her business a reality because she knows all too well there is no current product that meets this intense need for busy women. At Sloan, she met Anjali Banerjee and Mercedes Meceda, and together they be-gan plotting TechEx.

Huang has spent the bulk of her career in the online start-up world and is considered the consummate ideas person. After UCLA, she worked at an online beauty company, Glamazon.com, which gave users customized product tips based on their skin tone, col-oring, and facial dimensions. She then worked as an operations manager at an online nutrition company, Nutello, which she helped sell to Soapytime.com for $10 million. She serves as CEO, overseeing the day-to-day operations at TechEx.

Banerjee is a native Brit. A Harvard graduate, she worked at Morgan Goldman investment bank where she specialized in mezzanine finance. She gained international experience with that firm by working in Dublin for several years as well as from a brief stint in Paris. A pragmatic leader who's driven by numbers, Banerjee is TechEx's CFO. A vegan whose passions include marathon running and mountain biking, she is also actively involved in Women on Wall Street, a group for women in finance, and is on the board of trustees at The Kiddo's Lunch Place, a Boston nonprofit that helps children from low-income homes learn about healthy food choices.

Meceda, who majored in computer science at Stanford, is a former Dain consultant and has worked extensively in the health management field. She has a deep understanding of health problems associated

(*continued*)

SAMPLE MANAGEMENT SUMMARY

with obesity, including hypertension, heart disease, and diabetes, and has devoted her career to helping others adopt healthier lifestyles. A former yoga instructor, she also maintains a popular blog—Frequent-FlyerHealth—that's geared toward helping professional women who travel a lot for work stay healthy away from home by compiling lists of healthy restaurants, gyms, and spas by city, and offering short videos of yoga workouts that require minimal equipment and can be done in a hotel room. Her blog has more than 28,000 readers and she maintains a large Twitter following. Meceda—who is known in the industry as the ultimate taskmaster—is also secretary of the California Technology Together Board, a networking group for young people in the technology industry. She serves as CTO of TechEx.

Team experience: In addition to their prior professional work, the team members have had experience working together on a large project. The women, who met as MBA students at MIT Sloan, comprised the management team of Sloan's Entrepreneurial Ventures Club, the school's biggest student-run organization. During their time at the helm, the group established a For Women Only business plan competition that involved hundreds of female students from more than a dozen top business schools. Huang, Banerjee, and Meceda secured $200,000 in sponsorship funding from several Boston-based companies, including the Loyalty fund management group and the Life Is Sweet retailer. Today their competition is the largest women-only business plan contest in the world.

Other resources: The company works with a dietician, a psychologist who specializes in weight loss issues, and several personal trainers on a freelance basis. On legal issues, the management team works closely

(*continued*)

SAMPLE MANAGEMENT SUMMARY

with Berke & Kondell, P.A., a commercial law firm located in Boston. The organizational structure of the company will be very flat in the beginning, with each of the team members responsible for her own work and management.

Skills concerns: At this point, the biggest gap in management skills is marketing and sales. The team plans to remedy this by contracting with low-cost consultants and experts. Meceda has friends who have recently left Dain to launch their own firm focused on start-ups and who have expressed interest in working with TechEx for a significantly reduced fee as they start their own business. In addition, Jim Jacobs, a UCLA professor who served on the board of directors of Calorie Counters, is a family friend of Huang. He has offered to help the management team develop its marketing strategy at no cost. As the company grows, the team expects to take on an additional partner who specializes in marketing and sales.

Bringing Your Product to Market

Bringing Your Product
to Market

Providing detailed marketing and operations plans shows your readers that you've considered the large and small elements of your business's future daily life. These plans provide you with the opportunity to think through possible roadblocks and solutions and to demonstrate your understanding of the factors that both help make the business function and create value for stakeholders.

Operations plan: Articulating day-to-day business

The operations section of your business plan provides a general idea of the flow of everyday activities at your venture and the strategies that support them. This part should provide enough information to show that you understand and have planned for the daily execution of the business, but it should not be too technical or so comprehensive that the reader is either unable or unwilling to plow through it. A librarian can help you find the detailed information you need in reference books and trade journals. Trade associations are another good source for advice; they offer an array of resources to their members through newsletters and other publications as well as services such as conferences and seminars.

As you begin to develop your *operations plan*, remember that visual aids such as charts, graphs, and tables can help you present complicated information clearly. Here are some key considerations:

- *What is your breakeven point?* The point at which unit sales equal operating costs—the breakeven point—is perhaps the most important operational factor for a new venture or spinoff because it identifies the moment at which the business begins to make money. While financial projections of a prospective business are often just educated guesses, your audience will be looking for some indication of when they can expect a return on investment.

- *How will you source supplies?* What are the raw materials necessary to create your finished item? How much do they cost, who are your suppliers, where are they located, and why did you choose them?

- *What is your manufacturing or distribution process?* How will you transfer information and data? How can your business benefit from technological improvements in manufacturing? Are you able to organize your distribution systems in a low-cost way?

- *Where is your business based?* Have you chosen a favorable geographic location? Does your location offer proximity to customers or suppliers? Do the businesses located near you complement your offering or compete with it? Also, what is your office like? You might include a physical description of the site with pictures, layouts, or drawings of the location in the supporting document section of your business plan.

- *Who will work for you?* Do you have access to skilled employees? For instance, can you offer internships to recent college graduates who would provide the company with inexpensive labor in the present and experienced candidates to draw from for future positions? Is your labor pool stable? For example, are workers attached to the region and have they tended to remain there even during economic downturns? Are your prospective workers well equipped and do they have the educational backgrounds that your company needs? Or can you provide in-house training to ensure you have the expertise you need?

Marketing plan: Promoting your value proposition

Your *marketing plan* details how you intend to sell your product or service—that is, how you'll motivate customers to buy from you. Developing a coherent, comprehensive marketing strategy within your business plan helps you and your team pre-test ideas, explore options, and determine effective strategies for your venture's success. It also provides another opportunity to demonstrate how the mission and philosophy of your venture feeds your plan to drive sales and sustain customer loyalty. Readers—investors and corporate leaders alike—will want to see that you've thought carefully about how your specific marketing objectives will help you achieve your sales goals. Here are some key factors to consider as you create your marketing plan:

- *Concentrate on the opportunity.* What is the specific customer problem that your product or service solves? For example, you may be fixing a weakness in the competitors' services by offering product guarantees that aren't available elsewhere. Or perhaps you have a way to make diet soft drinks taste like their high-sugar counterparts. As you develop particular marketing strategies, consider the opportunity from the perspective of the customer: Does the product or service you're proposing make their lives better?

- *Focus on customers' buying behavior.* When, where, why, and how do consumers buy your product or service? What needs does it fulfill for them? What are your customers' priorities? What factors are important to them in choosing this type of product or service? Is it price? Quality? Value? Other benefits? For example, for time-pressed customers, service and convenience may trump price.

- *Determine each customer's value to your business.* Weighing the cost to acquire a customer against the long-term value of that customer helps you decide which marketing strategies are most appropriate. Do customers often buy your product as a consumable, such as lipstick or a notebook? Are you building an annuity business, such as a movie streaming subscription service that continues for years? Or are you selling a durable product that is purchased only occasionally during a lifetime, such as a washing machine or a car? Do you need to build brand loyalty, or is your product/service the only one that will fill customers' needs? Is the process of buying the product/service relationship oriented (like a loyalty program where you learn customer preferences and make suggestions about other items of interest)? Or is it transaction oriented (where you have limited communication with your customer and focus instead on efficiency or speed, such as a self-service kiosk at an airport terminal)?

- *Review your own objectives.* At what level of sales will you reach the breakeven point, and when do you anticipate achieving that level? After that, how long will it take to reach the next sales milestone? For example, you might intend to reach the breakeven six months after your initial sales, then increase sales by 10% per year, and then capture 10% of the target market in five years. What strategies can you design to fulfill these objectives?

Defining your marketing mix

Your marketing mix describes how you will achieve your marketing objectives. Your choices will determine: how you will make the target market aware of your product; how you will persuade customers within that target market to purchase it; how you will build customer loyalty; and whether you will achieve the projected return on sales. Your strategies here also determine how you will position your product in the market relative to your competitors' products. The most effective mixes reflect the classic "four Ps" of marketing: product, price, place (distribution), and promotion. Here is a breakdown:

- *Product and/or service:* Describe your
  product or service's form, functionality, special features, and architecture. How does it
  uniquely meet your target market's needs?
  What is your intellectual property, and how
  are you protecting it? What is your product
  development plan?

- *Price:* At what price point will you offer
  your product or service? Will there be an
  established price, or will it be tiered or variable depending on consumer demand? It's
  extremely difficult to guess how much people
  will pay for something, but a business plan
  must demonstrate that you have carefully
  considered your new venture's pricing scheme.
  Your pricing decisions depend on two factors:
  first, the price sensitivity of your market and
  the market's perceived value of your product;
  and second, your total costs and required profit

margin. Bear in mind that you may be able to adjust pricing to the needs of individual market segments or match high prices with unique service features.

- *Place (distribution):* How will your product be transported to the end user? What distribution channels will you use? How will you merchandise your product—in what kind of retail stores or locations? These decisions depend on the type of product, the costs of distribution, and customers' needs or demands.

- *Promotion:* How will you communicate with consumers and make them aware of your product? Depending on your available resources and your target audience, you'll need to select the right mix of approaches. Will you use word of mouth? (Satisfied customers singing your praises are a cheap, effective promotion, but unpredictable and difficult to control—

especially if the message turns negative.) Will you opt for sales promotions? (These might include relatively low-cost ways to reach a large number of customers via coupons, samples, and demonstrations.) Do direct sales make the most sense? (These pricier tactics range from individual sales calls to mass telemarketing and broadcast e-mailing.) Or is traditional advertising a better bet? (Paid persuasive messages, such as television commercials and print ads, tend to be expensive, but the payoff is a strong brand image and brand loyalty.)

SAMPLE MARKETING PLAN

TechEx's marketing plan is based on the recognition that the company has two distinct types of customers: end users who enroll in the weight loss program, and employers who offer TechEx services within their health and wellness programs. The latter market provides TechEx with a less expensive and more efficient way to reach the end user, as well as a lock on the primary distribution channels that will help erect barriers to entry from competitors.

Positioning

To end users, TechEx positions its service as a high-quality, personalized weight loss and fitness program for time-crunched professional women. The service facilitates targeted weight loss by synthesizing data on an individual's eating habits and physical activity and

(continued)

SAMPLE MARKETING PLAN

providing customized diet and exercise plans. Customers may also engage with a supportive community of fellow dieters online and at their own convenience, a service unlike those offered by most mainstream weight loss plans.

To companies, TechEx positions itself as an efficient and low-cost means to improve employee wellness. TechEx services may also be provided as a "perk" to employees who travel a lot for their jobs.

Pricing

TechEx's services are priced below the services of the company's closest rival, E-Fitfab. E-Fitfab offers a basic plan at $148 a month and an advanced plan at $298. TechEx's basic plan costs $125 per month; its most expensive plan costs $250 per month. The management team believes that pursuing a value pricing strategy is the best way to create a community of long-term users who will incorporate the service into their daily lives instead of viewing and using it as a luxury.

Fees are set on a sliding scale and reflect the level of service a customer desires. Upon joining, for instance, a customer might want to take advantage of all Te-chEx's services: weekly video sessions with dieticians, trainers, and behavior coaches. As the customer progresses through the program (and begins to lose weight), she may wish to scale back or ramp up those services. She may, for instance, wish to engage with her dietician only monthly, but increase the frequency of virtual sessions with her trainer. The basic program still provides the user with all her personal dietary and fitness data so she is able to create a self-directed

(*continued*)

SAMPLE MARKETING PLAN

weight loss plan. She has full access to community support at all levels of the program.

Customer value proposition and priorities

TechEx offers customers a superior benefit at a lower cost than rival programs. Customers are able to lose weight and get more fit in a way that's convenient to their lives. They lose weight safely under the watchful eyes of trained experts. They also receive social and emotional support from fellow dieters who understand the pressures that high-achieving women face in their personal and professional lives.

For corporate customers, TechEx is a cost-saver. It saves companies money through improved employee health (lower healthcare costs) and better retention (happier, less stressed employees). Employers and insurance companies are increasingly interested in the potential benefits of companies like TechEx. For example, several companies have made bulk purchases of pedometers to distribute to employees as part of their corporate health and wellness programs. Additionally, because prospective employees will recognize value in the service, offering TechEx to potential hires will become a means of differentiation and recruitment.

Distribution

Since the service is aimed at online users, the primary means of distribution will be the TechEx website. Customers will be able to join the service by paying with a credit card on TechEx's secure website. They will create an account with a username and password, allowing them to view their personal data anytime and anywhere. They will also be able to change their package preferences on a monthly basis.

(continued)

SAMPLE MARKETING PLAN

Advertising and promotion

Advertising and promotion will be a three-phase process that involves public relations (PR), web and print advertising, partner acquisition, and brand imaging. The management team plans to use outside advertising and PR agencies to ensure the creation and presentation of an overall coherent and professional message.

- *Phase I* is expected to last ten to twelve weeks and involves acquiring customers through print and web advertising. Web banner ads will be placed on sites that offer health and diet information, with a click-through link to the TechEx website. The TechEx home page will present information about service features, usage, and benefits, as well as an online registration form. Ads and site copy will educate prospective customers on the ease and convenience of TechEx's program in addition to offering testimonials from real women who have achieved significant weight loss based on a pilot program that will run prior to launch.

Phase I will also emphasize PR, paying special attention to supplying internet publications and the mainstream press with information about TechEx's unique service. Press kits with promotional material and free trials of fitfast will be sent to select reviewers and writers.

- *Phase II* will begin concurrently with Phase I, but it is expected to last up to six months. This phase will involve acquiring strategic partners. Primary targets are those companies that require long hours and heavy travel from their employees, including consulting firms and law firms.

(*continued*)

SAMPLE MARKETING PLAN

In addition, the management team will target companies that employ large numbers of women in high-level positions, such as accounting firms.

- *Phase III* begins immediately after the implementation of Phases I and II and will emphasize the branding of the service in diet and fitness magazines. It will also focus on generating additional media coverage through opinion pieces and blogs, written by TechEx's own Mercedes Meceda, that are geared at professional women who travel for their jobs. This type of promotion will be ongoing, and its primary purpose will be to strengthen the brand.

Projecting Financial Risk and Reward

Projecting Financial
Risk and Reward

Your financial plan shows your readers the current status and future forecasts of the company's financial performance. As noted in previous chapters, financial projections need not be exhaustive, but they must be addressed. The financial picture you paint here represents your best estimate of the risks involved and the return on investment, usually over a period of three to five years. Even if you have expert advice, crunching the numbers yourself is a worthwhile exercise. The gritty work of building an income statement and balance sheet will help you determine whether you will achieve your financial objectives.

Preparing your financial plan

Below are some key components of the *financial plan*:

- *Capital requirements:* How much money do you need to raise? How much do you expect from investors? And how do you intend to use the money? Whether your project is a business expansion or a new venture, be transparent.

- *Assumptions:* What are your expectations about growth rates in the industry and market? What are your assumptions about the internal components of the business, such as variable and fixed costs, growth rate of sales, cost of capital, and seasonal cash flow fluctuations? Your assumptions are the underpinnings of your financial plan, so they should be backed up with strong evidence and expert opinions.

Include a more detailed set of assumptions as an attachment.

- *Income statement:* Also known as your pro forma profit and loss statement, this document details your forecasts for your business for the coming three to five years. Here use numbers from your sales forecast, expense projections, and cash flow statement. Revenue, minus cost of goods sold, is your gross margin. TechEx's gross margin, for instance, is the money the company earns from subscriptions, less the cost of the fitfast monitors and the underlying technology. Revenue, less expenses, interest, and taxes, is net profit (also known as the "bottom line"). In TechEx's case, net profit is the money it earns minus the cost of the fitfast monitors and other technology, the salaries it pays to the management team, nutritionists, trainers, and others, taxes it owes, and the cost of the print and web ad campaigns.

- *Balance sheet:* This is an expression of the business's assets, equities, and liabilities at a specific point in time, and is generally prepared by your accountants.

- *Cash flow statement:* This shows the times of peak need and peak availability of money and indicates whether your company is successfully turning its profits into cash. If your new business is a start-up venture, pay close attention to cash flow in your financial plan. Although most people think of profits first, cash flow can be more important for a start-up. The cash flow statement shows in broad categories how a company acquired and spent its cash during a given period of time. Expenditures appear on the statement as negative figures, and sources of income appear as positive figures. The bottom line in each category is simply the net total of incoming and outgoing cash flow, and it can be either positive or negative. The broad categories are, generally, operating activities (cash generated by or used for ordinary business operations), investing activities (outgoing cash spent on capital equipment and other investments and incoming cash from the sale of such investments), and financing activities (outgoing cash used to reduce debt, buy back stock, or pay dividends and incoming cash from loans or from stock sales). The cash flow statement shows the relationship between net profit (from the income statement) and the actual change in cash that appears in the company's bank accounts. Many business planning software programs contain these formulas to help you make your projections.

Anticipating readers' concerns

Your financial plan provides a more complete picture of your proposal's future. As you craft this part of the business plan, consider your readers' perspectives.

The investment committee member, for instance, will want to know whether your venture can achieve the company's hurdle rate (the minimum rate of return expected of all projects). On the other hand, the venture capitalist (or even a smart family member) considering buying into your venture will want to know what kind of return on investment she will achieve. The bank or lender will want to know about the company's borrowing capacity and its ability to repay its debt when deciding whether to approve a loan.

Let's look at some of the other sections that typically comprise the financial plan.

Breakeven analysis

As noted earlier, the breakeven point is the pivotal moment when the business begins to be profitable. At what point do you expect the business to make money? Will it take six months or two years? The breakeven point for sales is calculated as follows:

$$\text{Breakeven} = \frac{\text{Fixed Costs}}{(\text{Sales} - \text{Variable Costs})/\text{Sales}}$$

Fixed costs are those expenditures that don't change as sales go up or down (for example, rent), and variable costs change in proportion to sales (for example, raw materials such as plastic or chemicals). Often, this calculation is included in the attachments to your business plan.

Assessing risk and reward

A risk/return graph can quickly show your readers the likelihood of failure, of achieving the predicted levels of return, and of phenomenal success (see figure 1). After all, measuring hypothetical investment returns without also measuring the amount of risk required to produce those returns is pointless.

The most likely outcome is indicated by the area under the bell curve, ranging from an acceptable

FIGURE 1

Risk/return graph

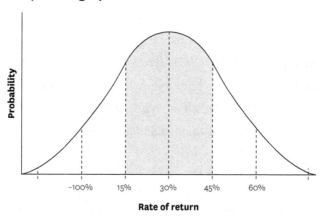

Source: Harvard ManageMentor® on Business Plan Development, adapted with permission.

(perhaps) return of 15% to the most likely return of 30% and a possible 45% rate of return. Depending on the fundamental riskiness of the venture, the investor will require different rates of return to balance the possibility of loss.

Anticipating financial returns

Investors also want to know the expected financial returns—typically either the return on investment (ROI) or the internal rate of return (IRR). For an internal project, the financial return should exceed the company's hurdle rate. For a risky start-up business, investors generally require a higher return to compensate for the higher level of risk of loss. To calculate the ROI, divide net operating income by total investments.

Net operating income/total investments = ROI

For example:

$45,000/$300,000 = 0.15 or 15% ROI

The higher the ROI, the more efficient the company is in using its capital to produce a profit.

Perhaps the simplest way to calculate IRR is to build a spreadsheet. That way, you can enter your own values and make adjustments as you go. For instance, to calculate an IRR of 50%—the return an investor might expect for a risky investment—use the following formula:

$$FV = \text{investment} \times (1 + 0.5)^n$$

(where *FV* is future value, *investment* is the dollar amount of the investment, and n is the number of years to receive the return).

Exit strategy

Your business plan should offer a candid proposal for the end of the process, according to William Sahlman. How will the investor ultimately get money out of the business, assuming that it is successful, even if only marginally so? Investors typically like to see companies that work hard to maintain and even increase a broad variety of exit options along the way. Your exit plan, for instance, may include taking your company public, merging your business with another one, or putting your company up for sale.

SAMPLE EXCERPT OF A FINANCIAL PLAN

Capital requirements

TechEx seeks to raise $250,000. According to current projections, the company believes this sum, together with $84,000 the company raised in its initial friends and family round of financing, will be sufficient to achieve its business plan. If the company is indeed able to raise this amount of money, the company will be able to fund all operations, marketing, and product development costs internally after the first six months of operation.

The company intends to use the $334,000 during the first six months of operation, as shown below:

- $100,000 for marketing

- $100,000 for system development and technology programming

- $60,000 for advances for contracts with dieticians, behavior coaches, and trainers

(continued)

SAMPLE EXCERPT OF A FINANCIAL PLAN

- $45,000 for working capital to fund future product development and promotion

- $29,000 for product design and creation (for the fitfast wearable monitor)

Summary financial projections

The financial plan portrays a projection of first-year sales of $11.74 million, gross margins in excess of 60%, and net margins of approximately 42% before tax. The company expects to be profitable after the first six months of operation and remain profitable thereafter. Other expenses are budgeted as a percentage of revenues according to similar industry ratios. Given these projected numbers, TechEx anticipates being profitable and cash flow positive within six months of launch. The results of the financial forecast are summarized:

	2015	2016	2017	2018	2019
Revenue ($)	11,750,000	33,754,258	39,642,675	43,606,943	47,967,636
Operating Profit ($)	4,926,073	14,518,828	16,971,337	18,731,825	20,669,785
Operating Margin	42%	43%	43%	43%	43%
Net Income ($)	4,926,073	14,518,828	16,971,337	18,731,825	20,669,785
Net Margin	42%	43%	43%	43%	43%

Assumptions

The financial projections are based on current industry estimates of diet and weight loss customers, primary and secondary market research data, and estimates of the TechEx's market penetration and sales growth. More detailed information on the assumptions can be found in the statements prepared for years 2015 through 2019, which incorporate projected income statements, balance sheets, and cash flows. Revenues include those resulting from registration of new

(continued)

SAMPLE EXCERPT OF A FINANCIAL PLAN

accounts and sales of additional services. Marketing and sales expenses include costs associated with advertising, PR, and promotions. The company will not carry any inventory and will operate with minimal overhead. No salary will be drawn by the management team in the first year.

Attachments
and Milestones

Attachments and Milestones

Supplemental information

Attachments come at the end of the business plan and provide additional information for the reader without weighing down the body of the plan. This is often where you append things such as: a complete set of financial statements (including assumptions, income statements, cash flow statements, and balance sheets); the technological specifications of the production plan; and the formal résumés for each member of the management team.

Milestones

A milestone plan gives your readers a timeline for your creation of a successful business. Develop an ambitious schedule that you can meet, while still giving yourself room to handle unexpected problems that may slow you down (such as raw materials that don't arrive on time or zoning snafus that tie up the permit for your new retail space). An aggressive yet realistic plan will impress your investors.

Include only major events (not each individual step) and choose milestones that can be clearly

FIGURE 2

Milestone timeline

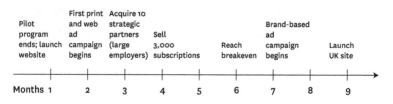

defined and easily measured—for example, "proto-type development," "installation of computer system," "market testing completed," or "first customer sale." Use generic dates, such as "month six" or "year one," rather than actual dates (see figure 2).

Conclusion

Conclusion

Writing a business plan is part of the process of preparing your business for success. But the document you create is not meant to be static. Once you've left the planning stages, regularly updating your business plan enables you to track your progress. Referring back to your business plan later in the process also helps you determine whether your original assumptions about the keys to your success are becoming realities. This provides valuable information—you'll be able to anticipate and respond to challenges before it's too late; you'll be able to update investors on progress; and, by verifying your original assumptions, you can continue to build your business.

Test Yourself

Test Yourself

B elow you'll find 10 multiple-choice questions to help you assess your knowledge of creating business plans. Answers appear after the test.

1. **A mission statement, which describes what your business is about and its philosophy and vision for the future, is best placed in the:**

   a. Executive summary
   b. Marketing plan
   c. Operations plan

2. **To impress potential investors, include detailed, month-by-month financial projections and forecasts for at least 10 years. True or false?**

   a. True
   b. False

3. **The balance sheet is:**

   a. Also known as a pro forma profit and loss statement.
   b. An expression of the business's assets and liabilities.
   c. A statement that shows the times of peak need and peak availability of cash flow.

4. **Weighing the cost to acquire a customer against the long-term value of that customer helps you:**

   a. Decide which marketing strategies are most appropriate.

   b. Better understand your competitors'
      sales strategies.

   c. Develop a realistic operations plan.

5. **The _____ is the minimum rate of return that is expected of all projects in a company.**

   a. Hurdle rate

   b. Gross margin

   c. Return on investment

6. **The management summary is best executed as an attachment that includes the résumés of your management team. True or false?**

   a. True

   b. False

7. **A financial tool that shows the point at which your business or venture is expected to neither be losing money nor making money is a:**

   a. Risk/Return graph.
   b. Cash flow analysis.
   c. Breakeven analysis.

8. **When researching the competitive outlook for your industry, it's wise to consider:**

   a. How much of a threat your competitors pose to your venture.
   b. Whether your competitors will aggressively block your entrance into the market.
   c. Who else might be able to observe and exploit the same opportunity that your new venture will capitalize on.
   d. All of the above.

9. The executive summary portion of your business plan is best written after you draft the rest of the plan. True or false?

   a. True
   b. False

10. When you're developing the milestones for your business plan, it's generally advisable to do all of the following *except*:

    a. Include only major events, not every individual step.
    b. Use actual dates.
    c. Leave time in the schedule for the unexpected.
    d. Develop an ambitious schedule you can meet.

Answers to test questions

1: **a.** An executive summary is a concise description of what your company is, where you want it to go, and why it will be successful. It gives readers an understanding of your proposal, and—importantly—captures their interest in your new venture, which is why it's the best place for a mission statement.

2: **b.** Be careful not to devote too much space to numbers and too little to the information that matters most to potential investors. Most reviewers are well aware that financial projections for a new company, especially comprehensive, month-by-month forecasts that extend for years and years, are little more than optimistic fantasies.

3: **b.** The balance sheet is an expression of a business's assets and liabilities. Assets include items like ready cash, accounts receivable (money owed to you), inventory, and real estate. Liabilities include things like debts from outstanding loans.

4: **a.** Weighing the cost to acquire a customer against the long-term value of that customer helps you decide which marketing strategies are most appropriate.

5: **a.** The company's hurdle rate is the minimum rate of return expected for all projects. If a project or venture doesn't pass the company's hurdle rate, it may not get approved or funded.

6: **b.** Many investors say that the management summary is one of the first sections of a business plan they read, so take special care to craft one that demonstrates how leaders will make the business work as a finely formed, dynamic unit.

7: **c.** The breakeven point is the pivotal moment when a business can begin to earn a profit. Readers want to know when and at what level of sales that will occur, and this form of analysis enables you to provide that information.

8: **d.** All of the above. Also consider whether rivals will recognize the attributes that set you apart and appropriate them for their own products or services.

9: **a.** The executive summary should be a concise presentation of the major points in your business plan, so it is best written last. If you were to write it at the beginning, you'd probably end up making significant revisions later.

10: **b.** It's generally not advisable to use hard dates in the milestone portion of your business plan because specific dates aren't always needed, and they leave you less wiggle room. Instead, use generic dates, such as six months or one year.

Learn More

Articles

Elsbach, Kimberly D. "How to Pitch a Brilliant Idea." *Harvard Business Review* (September 2003; product #R0309J).

Coming up with creative ideas is easy; selling them to strangers is hard. Entrepreneurs, sales executives, and marketing managers often go to great lengths to demonstrate that their new concepts are practical and profitable—only to be rejected by corporate decision makers who don't seem to understand the value of the ideas. Why does this happen? Having studied Hollywood executives who assess screenplay pitches, the author says the person on the receiving end—the "catcher"—tends to gauge the pitcher's creativity as well as the proposal itself. An impression of the pitcher's ability to come up with workable ideas can quickly and permanently overshadow the catcher's feelings about an idea's worth. To determine whether these observations apply to business settings beyond Hollywood, the author attended product design, marketing, and venture-capital pitch sessions and conducted interviews with executives responsible for judging new ideas. The results in those environments were similar to her observations in Hollywood, she says. Catchers subconsciously categorize successful pitchers as showrunners (smooth and professional), artists (quirky and unpolished), or neophytes (inexperienced and naïve). The research also reveals that catchers tend to respond well when they believe they are participating in an idea's development.

Magretta, Joan. "Why Business Models Matter." *Harvard Business Review* (May 2002; product #R0205F).

"Business model" was one of the great buzzwords of the internet boom. A company didn't need a strategy, a special competence, or even any customers—all it needed was a web-based business model that promised wild profits in some distant, ill-defined future. Many people—investors, entrepreneurs, and executives alike—fell for the fantasy and got burned. And as the inevitable counterreaction played out, the concept of the business model fell out of fashion nearly as quickly as the .com appendage itself. That's a shame, says Joan Magretta. As she explains, a good business model remains essential to every successful organization, from new ventures to established players. To help managers apply the concept successfully, she defines what a business model is and how it complements a smart competitive strategy. Business models are, at heart, stories that explain how enterprises work. Like a good story, a robust business model contains precisely delineated characters, plausible motivations, and a plot that turns on an insight about value.

It answers certain questions: Who is the customer? How do we make money? What underlying economic logic explains how we can deliver value to customers at an appropriate cost? Every viable organization is built on a sound business model, but a business model isn't a strategy, even though many people use the terms interchangeably. Business models describe how the pieces of a business fit together as a system. But they don't factor in one critical dimension of performance: competition. That's strategy's job. Illustrated with examples from companies like American Express, EuroDisney, Wal-Mart, and Dell Computer, this article clarifies the concepts of business models and strategy, which are fundamental to every company's performance.

Rich, Stanley R. and David E. Gumpert. "How to Write a Winning Business Plan." *Harvard Business Review* (January 2001; product #584X).

A well-conceived business plan is essential to the success of an enterprise. Whether you are starting up a venture, seeking additional capital for an existing product line, or proposing a new activity for a corporate division, you will have to write a plan detailing your project's resource requirements, marketing decisions, financial projections, production demands, and personnel needs. Too many business plans focus excessively on the producer, yet as this article shows, the plan must reflect the viewpoint of three constituencies: the customer, the investor, and the producer.

Sahlman, William A. "How to Write a Great Business Plan." *Harvard Business Review* (July–August 1997; product #97409).

Most business plans devote far too much ink to the numbers—and far too little to the information that *really* matters: the people, the opportunity, the context, and the possibilities for both risk and reward. This article builds on Sahlman's "Some Thoughts on Business Plans" and shows managers how to pose—and answer—the right questions as they prepare their business plans.

Books

Covello, Joseph and Brian Hazelgren. *Your First Business Plan: A Simple Question and Answer Format Designed to Help You Write Your Own Plan.* 5th ed. Naperville, IL: Sourcebooks, 2005.

This guide to writing a business plan includes a step-by-step process that focuses on the USA (Unique Selling Advantage). It includes a model of a complete business plan and a glossary of terms.

Harvard Business School Publishing. *Entrepreneur's Toolkit: Tools and Techniques to Launch and Grow Your New Business.* Boston: Harvard Business Review Press, 2004.

Starting an independent business is rife with both opportunity and peril. From the basics of writing a business plan to the challenges of financing a new venture, *Entrepreneur's Toolkit* is the essential resource for success. Topics include: navigating the world of venture capital funding, turning innovations into successful marketplace realities, establishing priorities and effective time management, and developing the sales and marketing programs needed for your venture.

Pinson, Linda. *Anatomy of a Business Plan: The Step-by-Step Guide to Building a Business and Securing Your Company's Future.* 8th ed. Tustin, CA: Out of Your Mind and Into the Marketplace, 2014.

The new edition has been revised to reflect the latest online and printed financial and marketing resources and current business plan practices. This business plan book is loaded with ready-to-use-forms and worksheets and five complete real-world business plans.

Sources

Harvard Business School Publishing. *Pocket Mentor: Creating a Business Plan*. Boston: Harvard Business School Press, 2007.

Harvard ManageMentor. Boston: Harvard Business School Press, 2002.

Sahlman, William A. "How to Write a Great Business Plan." *Harvard Business Review* (July–August 1997; product # 97409).

Index

Index

Index

Notes

Notes

Notes

Notes

Notes

Notes

Notes

Notes

Smarter than the average guide.

Harvard Business Review Guides

If you enjoyed this book and want more comprehensive guidance on essential professional skills, turn to the **HBR Guides series**. Packed with concise, practical tips from leading experts—and examples that make them easy to apply—these books help you master big work challenges with advice from the most trusted brand in business.

AVAILABLE IN PAPERBACK
OR EBOOK FORMAT
WHEREVER BOOKS ARE SOLD

- Better Business Writing
- Coaching Employees
- Finance Basics for Managers
- Getting the Mentoring You Need
- Getting the Right Work Done

- Managing Stress at Work
- Managing Up and Across
- Office Politics
- Persuasive Presentations
- Project Management

9 781633 695801